# WORD SOUP

## Coloring In For Adults

Relaxation and Positive Reinforcement

by

Vincent Van Gouache

# Word Soup

Word Soup is a book of word pictures that provide entertainment, positive reinforcement and relaxation for those of us who love expressing our creativity though coloring in.

Mindfulness and being positive can also help us feel better within ourselves.

Relax. Breathe deeply. Let your mind clear. Then, when you're ready, add colors that suit your mood to the patterns in this book. Let your mind wander, daydream.

A creative spirit exists within in each of us. Embrace it. — Vincent

ISBN-13: 978-1534620230
ISBN-10: 1534620230

# INDEX

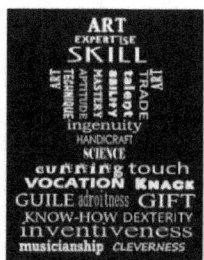
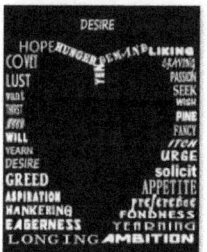
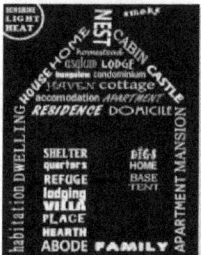
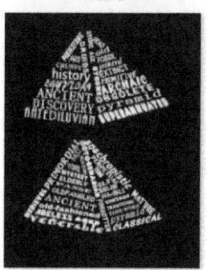
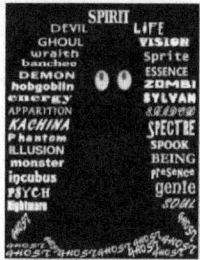
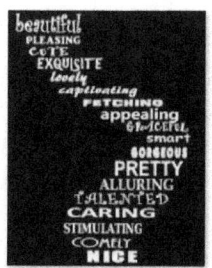
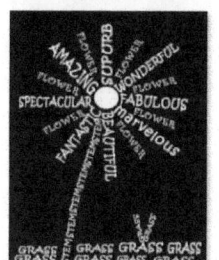
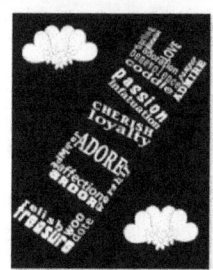
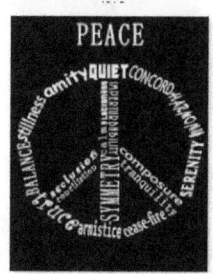
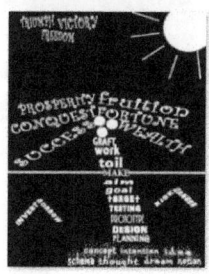
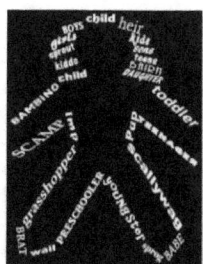
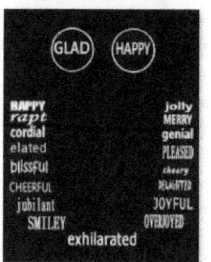
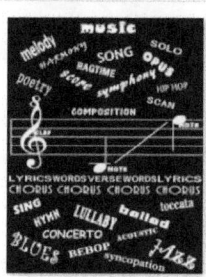
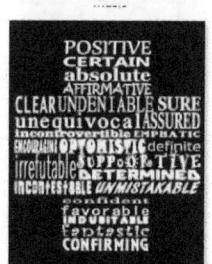
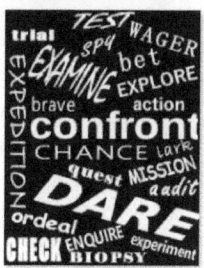
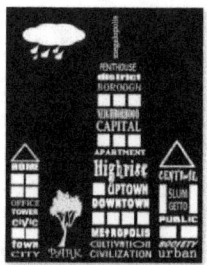
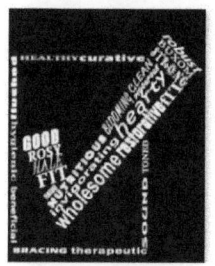
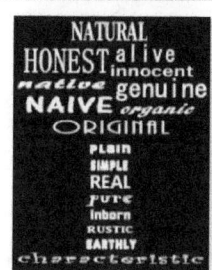
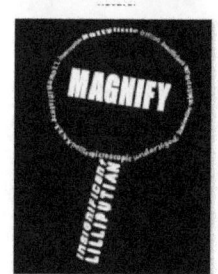
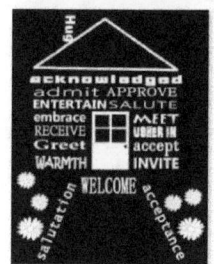

ART

EXPERTISE

SKILL

ART TECHNIQUE APTITUDE MASTERY ability talent TRADE ART

ingenuity

HANDICRAFT

SCIENCE

cunning touch

VOCATION KNACK

GUILE adroitness GIFT

KNOW-HOW DEXTERITY

inventiveness

musicianship CLEVERNESS

beautiful
PLEASING
CUTE
EXQUISITE
lovely
captivating
FETCHING
appealing
GRACEFUL
smart
GORGEOUS
PRETTY
ALLURING
TALENTED
CARING
STIMULATING
COMELY
NICE

child
BOYS heir
girls kids
sprout sons
teens
kiddo BAIRN
BAMBINO child DAUGHTER
toddler
SCAMP imp
PUP TEENAGER
grasshopper Scallywag
BRAT wait PRESCHOOLER youngster sprog BABE

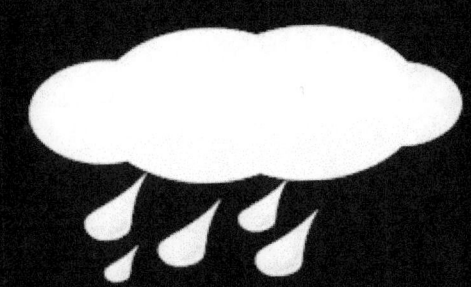

megalopolis

PENTHOUSE

district

BOROUGH

NEIGHBORHOOD

CAPITAL

APARTMENT

Highrise

HOME

OFFICE

TOWER

CIVIC

town

CITY

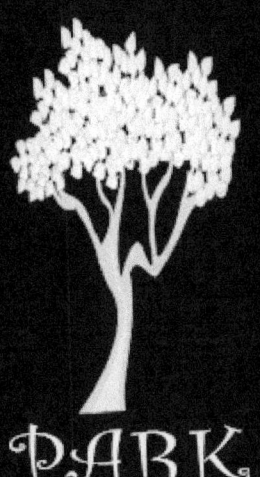

PARK

UPTOWN

DOWNTOWN

METROPOLIS

CULTIVATION

CIVILIZATION

CENTRAL

SLUM

GETTO

PUBLIC

SOCIETY

urban

# DESIRE

HOPE HUNGER YEN DEMAND LIKING

COVET CRAVING

LUST PASSION

want SEEK

THIRST WISH

need PINE

WILL FANCY

YEARN ITCH

DESIRE URGE

GREED solicit

ASPIRATION APPETITE

HANKERING preference

EAGERNESS FONDNESS

LONGING YEARNING AMBITION

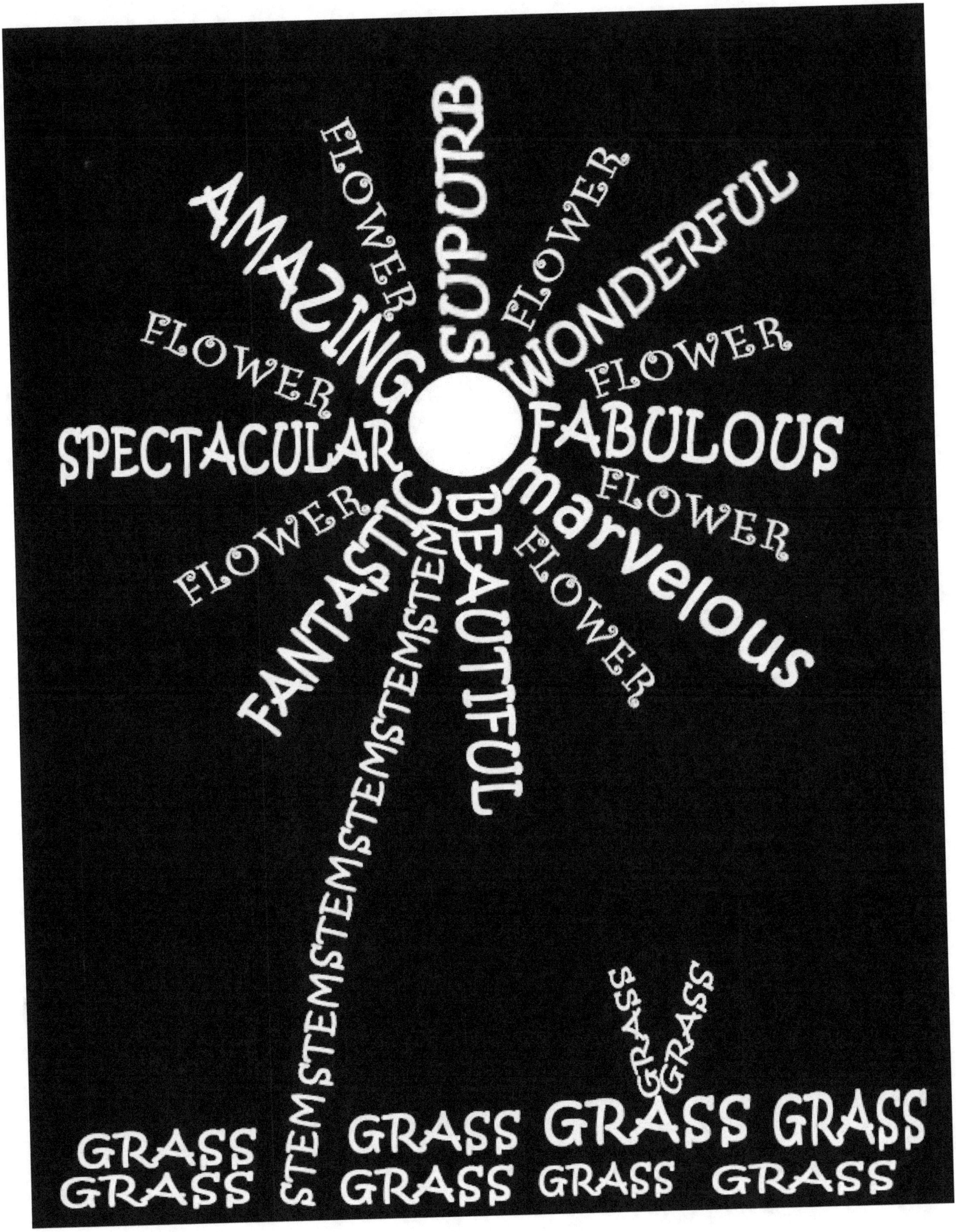
SUPURB
FLOWER
WONDERFUL
FLOWER
FABULOUS
FLOWER
marvelous
FLOWER
BEAUTIFUL
FANTASTIC
FLOWER
SPECTACULAR
FLOWER
AMAZING
FLOWER
STEMSTEMSTEMSTEMSTEMSTEMSTEM
GRASS
GRASS
GRASS GRASS GRASS GRASS
GRASS GRASS GRASS GRASS GRASS
STEM

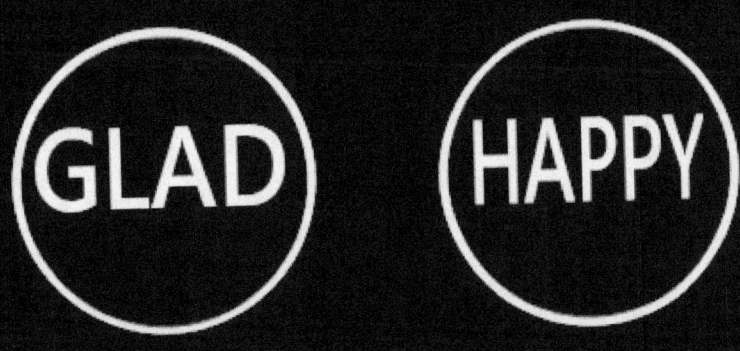

**HAPPY**
*rapt*
**cordial**
elated
blissful
CHEERFUL
jubilant
SMILEY

jolly
MERRY
genial
PLEASED
*cheery*
DELIGHTED
JOYFUL
OVERJOYED

exhilarated

HEALTHY curative

robust
BUXOM
STRONG
CLEAN
vigourous
BLOOMING
hearty
restorative FIT

flushing hygienic

GOOD
ROSY
HALE
FIT

FLUSHED
NUTRITIOUS
invigorating
wholesome restorative

SOUND TONED

beneficial

BRACING therapeutic

SUNSHINE
LIGHT
HEAT

smoke

NEST

HOME

CABIN

CASTLE

homestead

asylum LODGE

bungalow condominium

HAVEN cottage

accomodation APARTMENT

RESIDENCE DOMICILE

HOUSE

habitation DWELLING

APARTMENT MANSION

SHELTER
quarters
REFUGE
lodging
VILLA
PLACE
HEARTH
ABODE FAMILY

DIGS
HOME
BASE
TENT

darling
flirtation
adoration
benevolence
LOVE
coddle
pamper
ADMIRE
passion
infatuation
CHERISH
loyalty
ADORE
mesmer
pamper
affection
ardor
r s h i p
woo
relish
treasure
dote

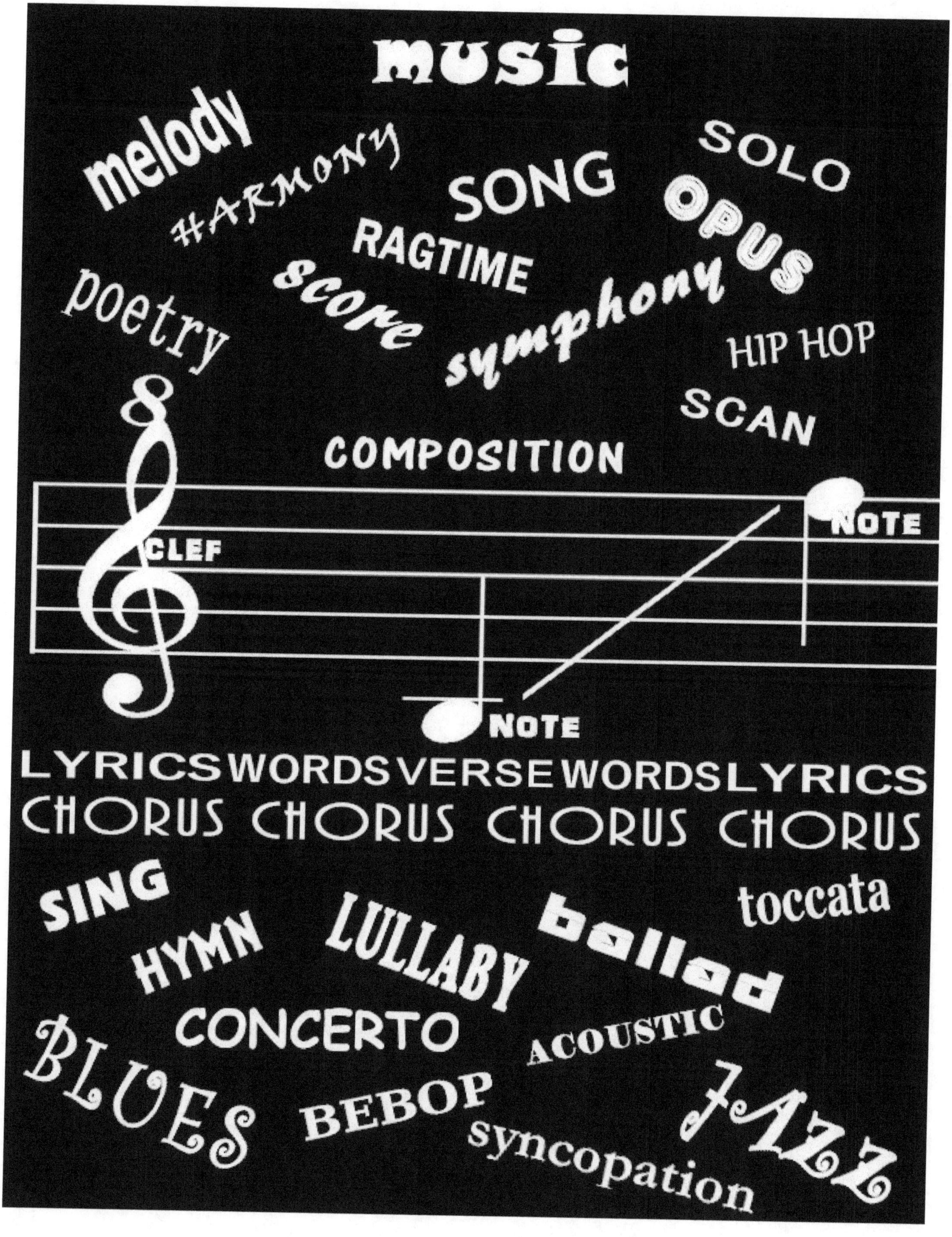
music
melody
HARMONY
SONG
SOLO
OPUS
RAGTIME
score
symphony
poetry
HIP HOP
SCAN
COMPOSITION
CLEF
NOTE
NOTE
LYRICS WORDS VERSE WORDS LYRICS
CHORUS CHORUS CHORUS CHORUS
SING
toccata
HYMN
LULLABY
ballad
CONCERTO
ACOUSTIC
BLUES
BEBOP
JAZZ
syncopation

# NATURAL
# HONEST alive
## innocent
*native* genuine
# NAIVE *organic*
## ORIGINAL

**PLAIN**

**SIMPLE**

# REAL

*pure*

**inborn**

RUSTIC

**EARTHLY**

*characteristic*

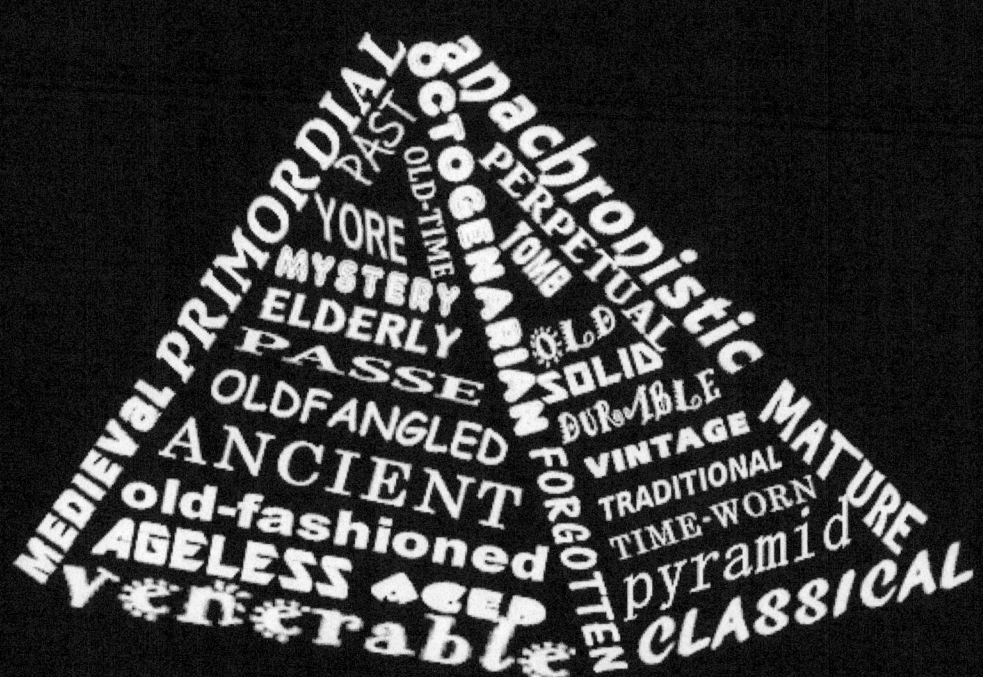

# PEACE

QUIET
amity
CONCORD
stillness
HARMONY
BALANCE
IMPERTURBABILITY
placidness
calm
PLACIDNESS
SYMMETRY
composure
tranquility
SERENITY
seclusion
conciliation
truce
armistice
cease-fire

# POSITIVE
## CERTAIN
## absolute
## AFFIRMATIVE
# CLEAR UNDENIABLE SURE
# unequivocal ASSURED
## incontrovertible EMPHATIC
## ENCOURAGING OPTOMISTIC definite
## irrefutable SUPPORTIVE
## DETERMINED
## incontestable UNMISTAKABLE
## confident
## favorable
## INDUBITABLE
## fantastic
## CONFIRMING

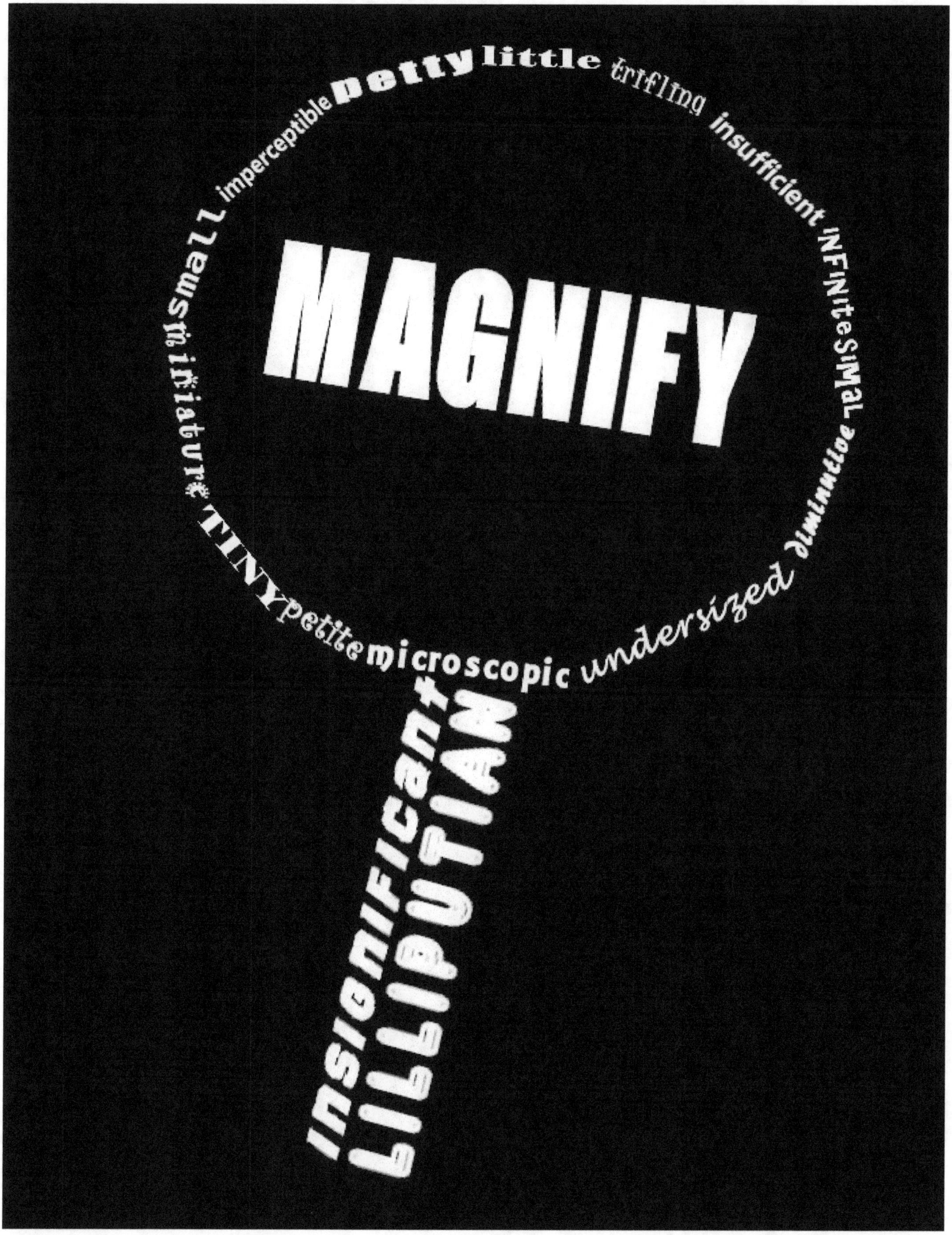
MAGNIFY
imperceptible
petty
little
trifling
insufficient
INFINITESIMAL
diminutive
undersized
microscopic
petite
TINY
miniature
small
insignificant
LILLIPUTIAN

SPIRIT

DEVIL

LIFE

GHOUL

VISION

wraith

Sprite

banchee

ESSENCE

DEMON

ZOMBI

hobgoblin

SYLVAN

energy

SHADOW

APPARITION

SPECTRE

KACHINA

SPOOK

Phantom

BEING

ILLUSION

presence

monster

genie

incubus

SOUL

PSYCH

Nightmare

GHOST GHOST GHOST GHOST GHOST GHOST GHOST GHOST

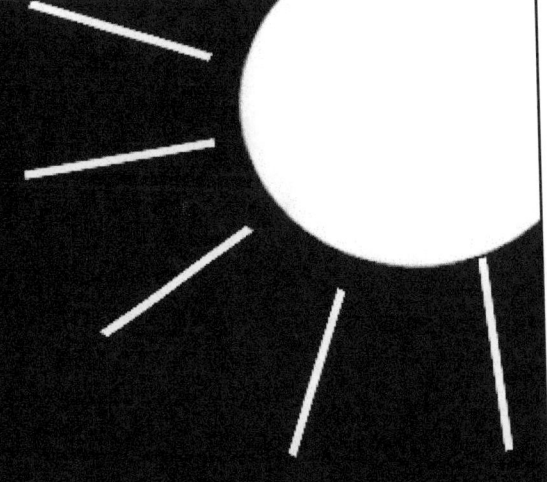

TRIUMPH VICTORY
FREEDOM

PROSPERITY fruition
CONQUEST FORTUNE
SUCCESS WEALTH

GRAFT
work
toil
MAKE

aim
goal
tarGet
TESTING
PROTOTYPE
DESIGN
PLANNING

INVEST BORROW

RISK DANGER

concept intention idea
scheme thought dream notion

TEST

trial

WAGER

SPY

EXAMINE

bet

EXPLORE

EXPEDITION

brave

action

confront

CHANCE lark

quest MISSION

audit

DARE

ordeal

CHECK ENQUIRE experiment

BIOPSY

Hug

acknowledged

admit APPROVE

ENTERTAIN SALUTE

embrace MEET

RECEIVE USHER IN

Greet accept

WARMTH INVITE

salutation WELCOME acceptance

# Bonus Patterns

I've included some bonus patters to give you an idea of the mandalas and other geometric patterns I love to create for those with a creative streak. Enjoy.

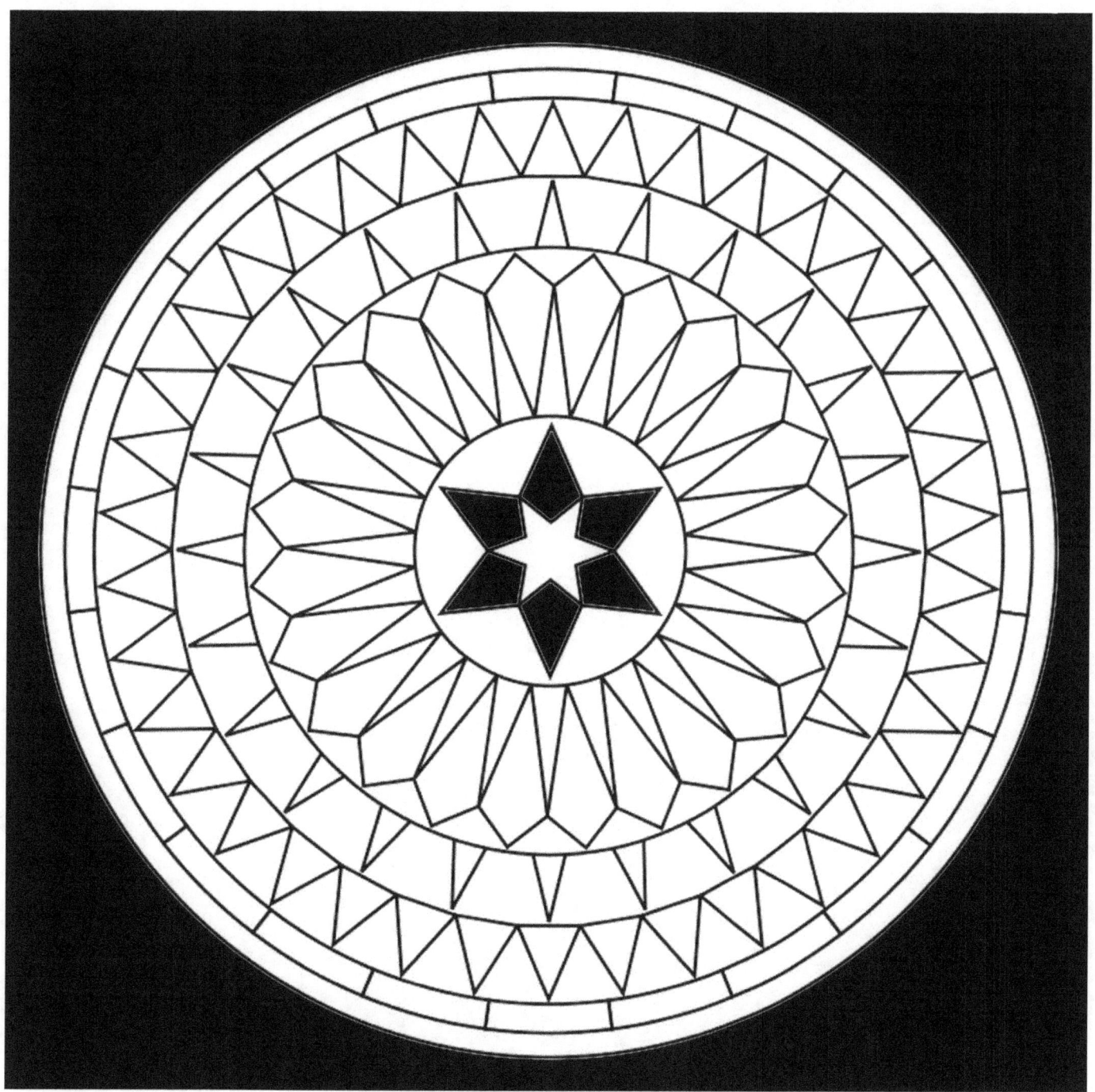

From Midnight Mandalas

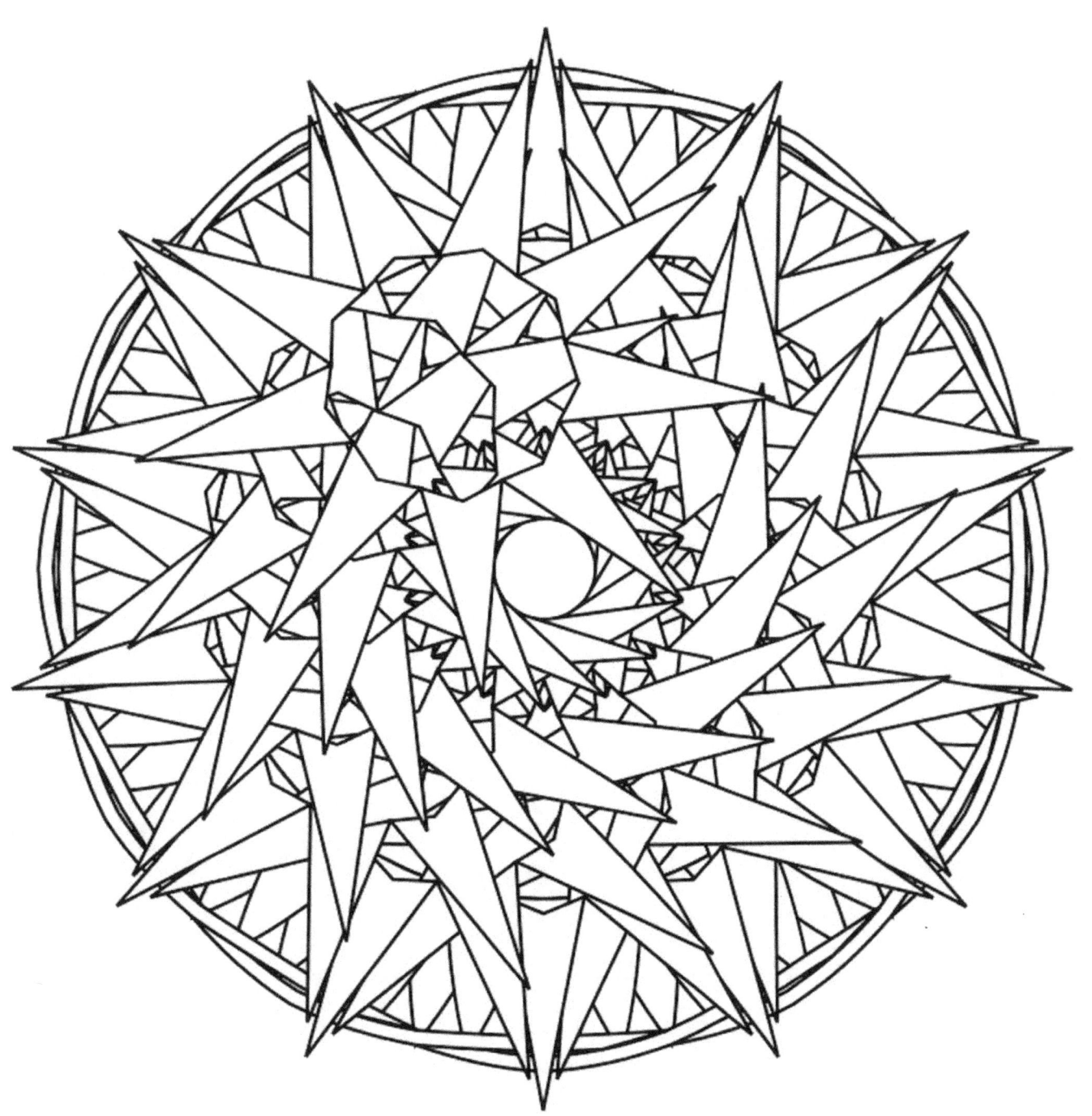

From Mandala Mania

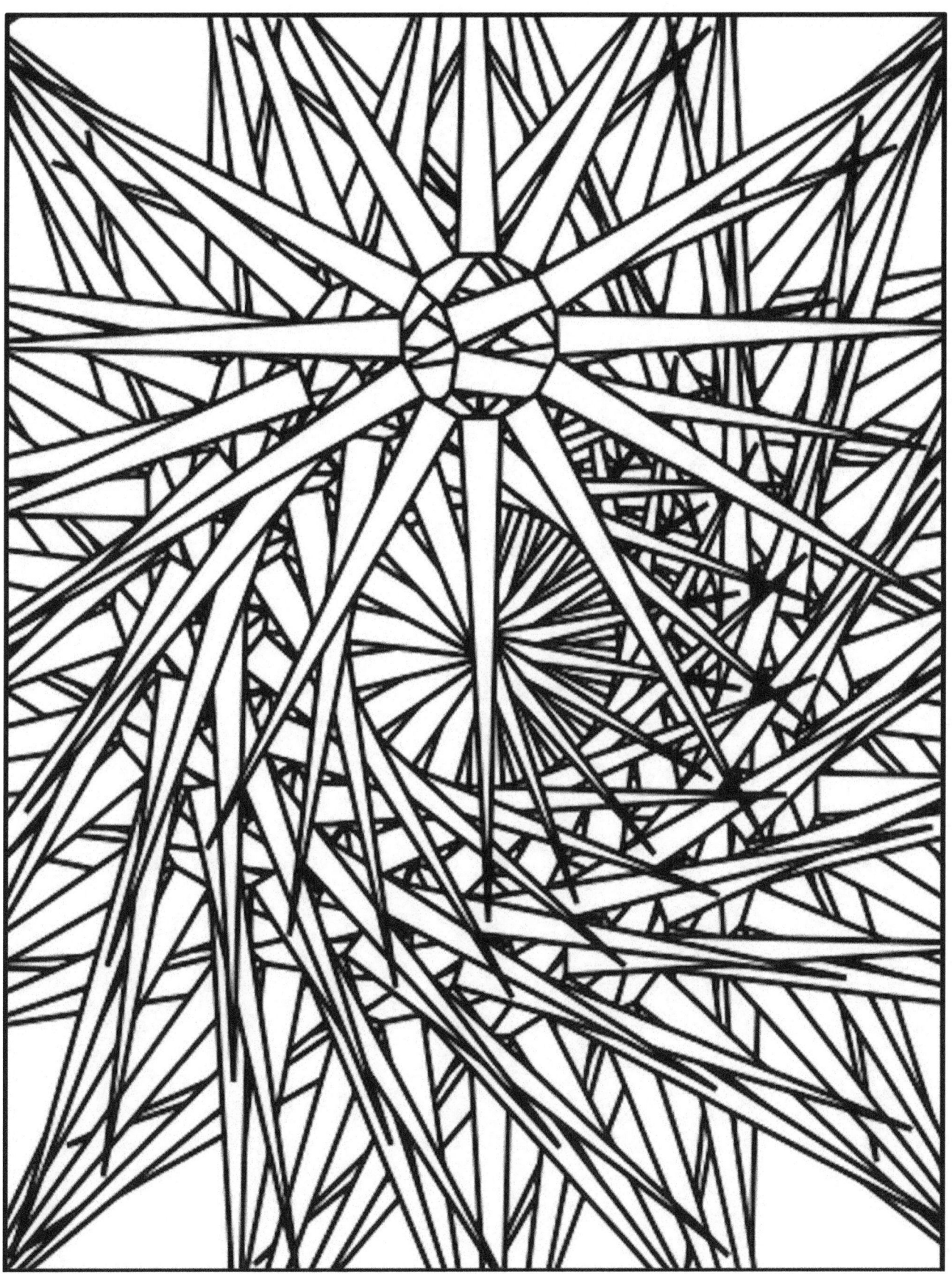

From Creative Coloring - Geometrics

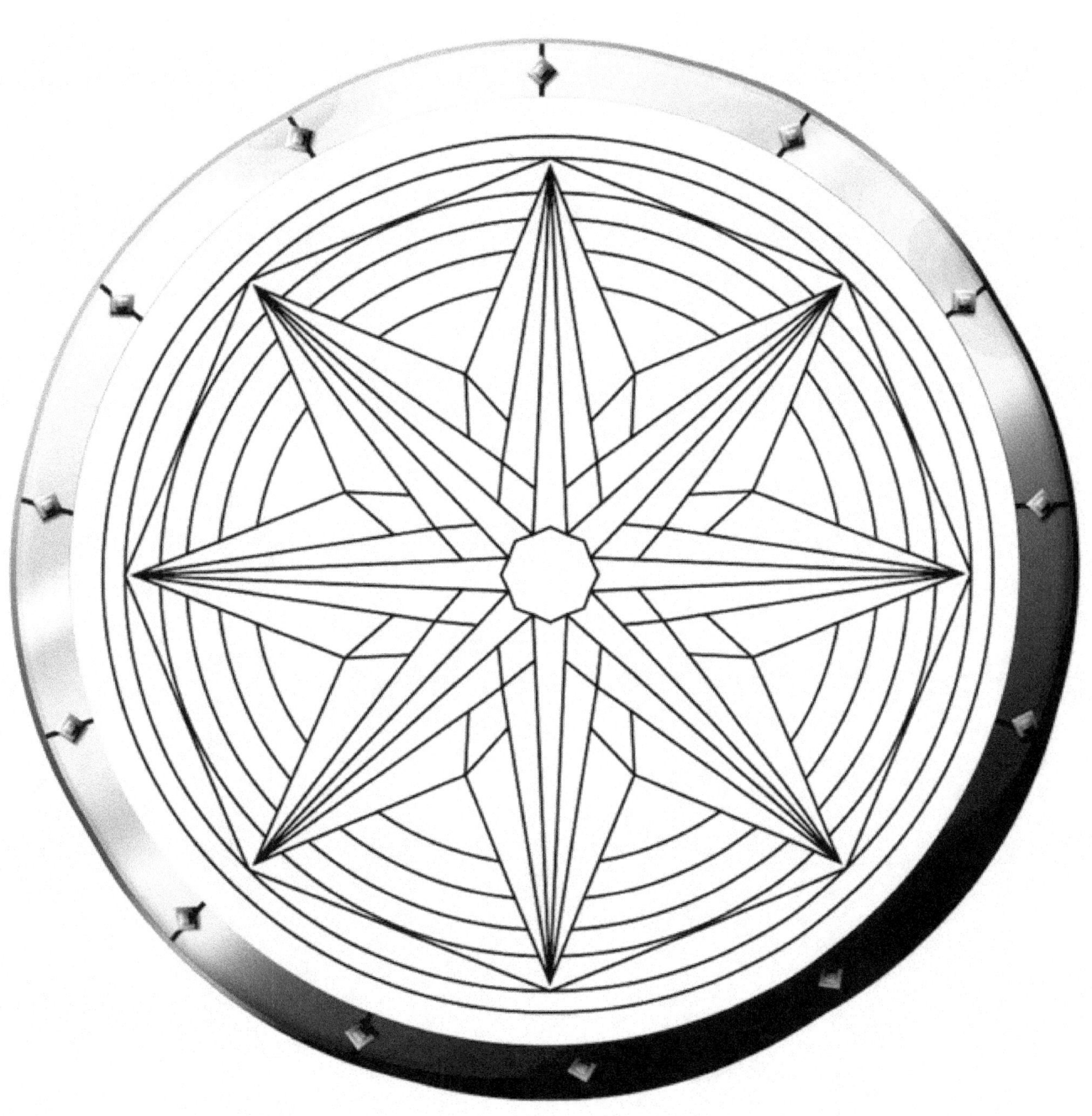

From Warrior Shields

# Other Coloring Books by
# Vincent Van Gouache

All available from Amazon

Psycho Color

Psycho Color 2

Mandala Mania

The Psycho Color Collection (3 books in 1)

The Book of Calm

Relax

Creative Coloring - 100 Mandalas

Creative Coloring - Geometrics

Warrior Shields

Midnight Mandala Mania

Moonlight Mandalas